The Ten Commandments Take 2

RAY WOHLFARTH

DEDICATION

To God, who stood by me despite my efforts to push him away. I have been blessed with a loving family and incredible grandchildren. This is a tongue in cheek look at what the Ten Commandments would look like if they were written today. I believe God has a sense of humor or he would not have invented the aardvark.

CONTENTS

THE MEETING

As usual, forty-one-year-old Liz Walker was multitasking while driving. The lead lawyer for the local chapter of the ACLU or American Civil Liberties Union was reading an email while driving. She didn't see the light turned red and blew right through at 50 miles per hour. Her old Toyota Corolla didn't stand a chance against the municipal garbage truck. Liz found herself in front of a tall white gate with the letters P and G in cursive in the center. Standing in front of the gate was a man holding an iPad. The man wore all white including shorts, a white button-down shirt, and white Hey Dude shoes.

Approaching the man, she was about to speak, and the man said, "Hello, Liz."

"You know me? Who are you?" she asked, a bit confused.

"My name is Peter, not Pete, Petey, or P Man." He had short, buzzed hair and a close-cropped beard.

Nodding, she asked, "Where am I?"

"You're kidding, right? I thought the Pearly Gates gave it away," he said pointing to the P and G letters.

"Pearly Gates?"

Continuing, she asked, "I'm in Heaven? I stopped believing

in this years ago."

"Yeah, we know. Congrats on making the cut," he said.

"The cut?"

"You're up here rather than being down there," he said pointing down.

Continuing, he said, "Anyway, the Big Guy wants to see you."

"The Big Guy?"

"You know, God," he said.

"Oh, OK. When you said big guy, I thought you were talking about Chris Farley. He's like a second cousin," she said.

"Nope, the other Big Guy. Follow me," he said, and she did.

"Wait, I thought we were greeted by a family member when we got here."

"Naw, that only happens on TV," he said.

"I thought all angels had long hair and beards," she mused.

Looking at her, he said, "We do have barbers and hair stylists up here."

They knocked at a big wooden door, and it opened. Inside, she saw four angels, complete with halos. "These are God's assistants," Peter informed her.

She saw a man with a long beard in the next room who looked like one of the Duck Dynasty actors. He briskly walked to her and shook her hand, "Liz, hi, I'm God. Nice meeting you." Leading her to the couch, he sat opposite her. She noticed he wore new Birkenstock sandals, the model she planned to purchase next week.

"You're probably wondering why I wanted to see you," he said, and she nodded.

"I am curious."

"Well, we are thinking of updating the Ten Commandments. They were written long ago when there was fire and brimstone, you know, the whole wrath of Me thing. We want something which can resonate with the younger people on Earth, something they would understand," he said.

"Why me?" she asked.

"Well, you don't take crap from anyone. You would give me your honest opinion. Up here, everyone is like, Yes God, As you wish God. Besides, you are a recent arrival and understand what's going on down there," he said.

"So, what should I call you?"

Shrugging his shoulders, he said, "God."

"You don't have a first name like Jesus?" she asked.

"No, we wanted a way to differentiate him from me. I didn't want both of us turning around when someone called God, which still happens a lot," he said.

"My mom and I share the same name. Someone would call out Liz, and we would both answer," she said nervously, rubbing her hands together and God nodded with a smile.

"Will you help?" God asked, and she nodded.

"Great, here is a copy of the Ten Commandments. I assume it's been a while since you read them. I'll let you get settled in up here and we can get started in a few days," he said handing her a sheet of parchment paper with the Ten Commandments written in cursive.

I am the Lord thy God, who brought thee out of the land of Egypt, out of the house of bondage. Thou shalt not have strange gods before me. Thou shalt not make to thyself a graven thing, nor the likeness of anything that is in heaven above, or in the earth beneath, nor of those things that are in the waters under the earth. Thou shalt not adore them, nor serve them.

A few days later, Liz once again, found herself in God's office.

"Let's start with the First Commandment," she said. Suddenly, she heard the four assistant angels shout in unison,

I am the Lord thy God, who brought thee out of the land of Egypt, out of the house of bondage. Thou shalt not have strange gods before

me. Thou shalt not make to thyself a graven thing, nor the likeness of anything that is in heaven above, or in the earth beneath, nor of those things that are in the waters under the earth. Thou shalt not adore them, nor serve them.

 Liz watched God's eyes rolling.

"They do that every time, so let's not say it out loud again, shall we?" he whispered, and she nodded.

Liz rubbed her chin, silently reading the first commandment, and asked, "Can I be honest here?"

"Of course, besides, I would know if you weren't," he said.

"Oh right. I'll start with the first sentence. Most people under thirty couldn't find Egypt on a map if their life depended on it. We should remove it," she said, and the angels gasped audibly. It was weird how their voices synced.

"Hey, could you give us the room? I think there is a wine tasting from the different waters of the world Jesus converted," God said, and the angels left.

"They do love their wine, now where were we?" he asked.

"I don't remember the first commandment being so long. Granted, it's been a while since I read it," she said.

Shaking his head, God said, "Some of the Catholics decided to shorten it. You probably remember the shortened version, "I am the Lord thy God. Thou shall not have strange gods before me."

Liz nodded and asked, "How does the same commandment differ like that?"

"That's exactly why I asked you to do this. I thought the commandments were perfectly clear. I wrote them on stone tablets and still they got it wrong. How do you get that wrong?" God asked and Liz shrugged her shoulders.

"What about the Egypt part? Liz asked.

"I agree with the Egypt statement. It is a little dated," he said.

"And the part about bondage, it has a much different connotation now than when this was written, if you know what I mean. I think we should remove it," she said.

"But I did save them from bondage, slavery," he said passionately.

"Slavery, don't bring that up. It's such a hot topic on Earth," she said passionately, and He nodded.

Liz looked at him and said, "People on earth have a saying, what have you done for me lately? You are talking about something that happened thousands of years ago."

"I'm beginning to see that," he said.

"Which brings me to, you shall have no other gods before Me."

"What's wrong with it?" He asked, his arms folded across his chest.

"Well, it's not a good look. It makes you seem needy and jealous. If humans wanted a needy, jealous guy, they could look at any of the men in their contact list," she said.

"I never thought about it; what do you suggest?" he asked.

"It's always better to under promise and over-deliver," she said, and he nodded.

"How about You've tried the rest; now try the best! I saw it somewhere," he said.

"It's on every pizza delivery box."

"That's where I saw it. OK, what are you thinking?" he asked.

"Shall is pretty strong. Remember, you are talking to people who hate being told what to do, and you did give us Free Will to choose," she said, and he nodded.

"How about God should be the top contact in your life," she said.

Continuing, "It exudes self-confidence without sounding needy or jealous."

"I like it, Liz, thanks," he said.

"I have a question for you. If Jesus was crucified on Friday and raised from the dead three days later, wouldn't that make Easter a Monday?" Liz asked.

"Never really thought about it," he said, rubbing his chin.

"Friday to Saturday is one, Saturday to Sunday is two, and Sunday to Monday three. I'm a lawyer, and details matter to me," Liz said counting with her fingers.

"Perhaps it's one of the mysteries in the church," God said smiling and stood.

"Hey, a few of us are bowling over Kansas; care to join us? Chris Farley will be there. He throws an incredible bowling ball. Should create a good storm," he said.

"You mean thunderstorms are really caused by bowling in heaven?" she asked, smiling, and he nodded.

1st Commandment Ver 2.0 First draft

God should be the top contact in your life.

Second Commandment

Thou shalt not take the name of the Lord thy God in vain.

Liz caught sight of herself in the full-length mirror and smiled. Ever since she arrived, she hasn't had one bad hair day. On her feet were the new Birkenstock sandals. She always wanted to experience all that life or in this case afterlife would offer. She was quickly getting used to Heaven and realized if you thought about something, it would appear. Her two favorite activities so far were visiting Deep Creek Lake, where her family vacationed yearly, and playing Up Here or Down There. It was a trivia game hosted by Bob Barker where he would say the name of a person who died, and you would have to guess if they were up here, in Heaven, or down there, in Hell.

When she arrived in Heaven, God asked her to help rewrite the Ten Commandments to appeal to younger generations.

Today, she was to meet with God to discuss the Second Commandment. Liz walked into the garden and saw God standing before an easel. He was painting a picture of a hummingbird. She admired the beauty of the painting, and God asked, "What do you think?"

"Remarkable," she said, and he smiled. They sat at a table, and he poured Earl Grey tea for both.

"How's it going?" he asked.

"Great. It's amazing here," she said.

"Well, we don't call it Heaven for nothing," he said, smiling. He had the most incredible smile.

"As far as the Second Commandment, I never realized there were so many Bible variations," she said, sipping the tea.

"I know, and each version is different. It must be so confusing," he said, and she nodded.

Liz looked at the table and smiled. There was a plate of shortbread cookies, just like her grandmother made when she was a child. "These look like my Grandma Mary's," she said.

With a twinkle in his eyes, God said, "I got the recipe from her." She took a bite and sighed; a tear formed in her eye.

Glancing at her notes, she said, "The King James bible says the second commandment is, *You shall not make for yourself a carved image, or any likeness of anything that is in Heaven above, or that is in the Earth beneath, or that is in the water under the Earth. You shall not bow down to them or serve them, for I the LORD your God am a jealous God, visiting the iniquity of the fathers on the children to the third and the fourth generation of those who hate me, but showing steadfast love to thousands of those who love me and keep my commandments."*

"A bit over the top, huh?" God asked and took a bite from the cookie.

Smiling, she said, "Just a bit. The Catholics obviously didn't get this version. Every church has a crucifix with a carving of Jesus on the cross. I used to have a crucifix necklace when I was young. And their version of the second commandment is "Thou shall not take the name of the Lord thy God in Vain. How could they be so different?" she asked.

"It's like that party game when you whisper a story to one person, and by the time it gets to the last person, the story is much different than the original." he said. God has the driest sense of humor, she thought.

"Just curious, how did you fit all these words on two small stone tablets?"

Holding his thumb and forefinger close, he said, "Really small font."

Liz asked "So, what would you like this commandment to say? What message would you like?"

God looked up and away and said, "I would like them not to ignore me or take me for granted."

Smiling, she asked, "How about I am your God, show me a little respect."

"I like it," he said.

"Can I ask you something which has bugged me since I was a teen?"

"Of course," he said.

"Was Elizabeth really in her eighties when she had her baby John?"

"88," he said.

"So, she was 90 when John was in his terrible twos. What were you thinking? No offense meant."

God chuckled and said, "No offense taken. She wanted a baby, so I gave her what she prayed for."

Liz asked, "How did her husband feel about being a father that late in life?"

"It did not go over well. Zecharia was not happy," he said.

"Is that why your angel Gabriel took away his ability to speak until after John was born?" Liz asked.

"It was a bit of an overreaction, but we were all tired of his jabbering. He changed how he felt once John arrived," God said.

"Wanna hear a joke?" she asked and God nodded.

"I heard this joke by a comedian, Wolfie. The joke is, "Of all the miracles written in the bible, the biggest miracle was never mentioned. How did Jesus find four guys named Mathew, Mark, Luke, and John in Israel?" she said.

God laughed loudly and said, "That's funny. You will have to tell Jesus that joke. He will love it."

"One last question, if I may, did you really create a flood that lasted for forty days, and was there an ark?" she asked.

"That wasn't me. It was global warming," he said, and her eyebrows raised.

"Just kidding. It was me. It was a crazy time. I was a different god then," he said, and she nodded.

"Well, Liz, I have to go. Jesus and I are going fishing," God said.

"A little father-son bonding," she said, and he nodded.

"Thanks for all your help."

"You're welcome," she said, and He was gone. Liz looked across the table and saw her grandmother, Mary, seated across from her.

2nd Commandment Ver 2.0 First draft

I am your God; show me a little respect.

Third Commandment

You shall keep holy the Sabbath Day

Liz wore a ball cap with the Heaven's Angels baseball team logo, a souvenir from last night's baseball game where the Angels played Major League Baseball's All-Stars. Today, God invited her aboard his sailboat, "Better than Walking on Water."

God held her hand as she stepped aboard, and said, "Weather is supposed to be perfect for sailing today."

"Isn't the weather always perfect up here?" she asked.

"It depends on your definition of perfect. Some people pray for clear weather during an outdoor event, and others pray for rain if they are farmers, all in the same area." God said, and the boat pulled away.

"Never thought about it. Guess you can't please everyone,"

she said.

"Welcome to my life," he said, smiling.

"How was tea with your grandma?"

"Incredible, thanks for setting it up," she said with a wide smile.

After two hours of sailing, the boat stopped, and they sat at a table. Fresh fruit appeared on the table, including bananas, oranges, and grapes. Two cheeseburgers appeared, as well as two chocolate milkshakes.

"Nice."

"Thanks," he said.

"What's on your mind, Liz?" he asked.

"Ear hair," she said.

"Didn't expect that."

"How come guys get hair growing from the ears as they age? I used to trim my dad's and always wondered about it. He had no hair on his head but plenty in his ears," she said.

"There was a valid reason for it. I realized the sense of hearing would fade as the body aged and knew hearing aids would not be invented until 1898. Some of the top engineers and physicians here and I met and discussed what could be done. The consensus was sound could be captured by ear hairs and transmitted to the ear. Sadly, all the hairs did was filter out the voices of family members, especially the spouse. See, even I make mistakes," he said and Liz chuckled.

"I wouldn't consider it a mistake. Think of it like a work in progress," she said and he smiled.

"Speaking of hairs, what's the deal with the hairs on our toes?" she asked.

"A designer who passed told me she thought hairs on the toes would provide color to the feet. Several others agreed so we gave it a go. Apparently, she thought feet were ugly. I never realized how many people think feet are ugly," he said.

"You can count me in that camp. So, there is no purpose to them? Some believe it's left over from when we evolved from apes," she said.

"You did not evolve from apes," he said loudly. "Sorry, that was the Old Testament God rearing its head. I get so tired of hearing about evolution. Charles Darwin is such a condescending putz. I avoid him at all costs. If you evolved from apes, why are there still apes? It's a sore spot for me," God said.

"Point taken," she said, making a mental note never to bring up evolution again.

"So, the third commandment, You shall keep holy the Sabbath Day," she said, and he nodded.

"There used to be a time when the Sabbath Day was observed. Stores were closed. People had family dinners on Sundays. Families would attend church together. Now, they run from one soccer game to another, from one baseball practice to the next. And then there is football. The NFL even jokes about how Sundays belong to them now. It breaks my heart," he said.

"Because they forget about you?" Liz asked.

"It's not only me. Sure, I appreciate it when someone thanks me, but it's much more than that. I want people to appreciate what they have. Take a few minutes to be thankful for their family, their health, and their lives. Humans were not meant to operate seven days a week. They need some downtime," he said.

"How about this, Before you start your Sunday, take a few minutes to be thankful for your lives. A shoutout to God would be nice occasionally," Liz asked, and God nodded.

"I couldn't have said it better," he said.

"One more question: While researching for today's meeting, I found out the Jews have over 600 commandments. Is it true?" she asked.

God rolled his eyes and said, "613 commandments. They are so over the top."

"I was wondering how many stone tablets Moses would have to bring down from the mountain for that many commandments. Why so many?"

Laughing, God said, "They are a stubborn lot, pardon the pun. I had them wander the desert for forty years, hoping to change their attitude, but no. They had way too much time on their hands, and that's where the 613 commandments came from."

3rd Commandment Ver 2.0 First draft

Before you start your Sunday, take a few minutes to be thankful for your lives. A shoutout to God would be nice occasionally.

Honor thy father and thy mother.

Liz looked in the mirror and checked her appearance before leaving the house. Her house in Heaven was a small log cabin next to a lake. Often, animals were grazing in her yard. She also started a garden and discovered she had a green thumb. Walking outside, Liz sniffed deeply and smiled; she loved the smell of honeysuckle. Today, she and God were hiking to discuss the fourth commandment.

"Morning, Liz," God said.

"Morning God, how are you?"

"A little troubled today," he said.

"What's wrong?"

"All the killings on Earth, Humans are slaughtering each other, and there seems to be such a divide," he said.

"I know. Everyone is so angry all the time," she said.

"I don't get it," he said.

They walked for about an hour and came to a clearing. A table appeared with sandwiches, iced tea, and cookies. As they were seated, God asked, "No questions today, Liz?"

"You sent your son to earth knowing he would die," she said tentatively.

"Everyone dies on earth," he said.

"But your son," she said softly.

"Hardest decision I ever made," he said.

"Couldn't you have done something a little less drastic?" she asked.

Shrugging his shoulders, he said, "I tried the tough love: plagues, locusts, famine. Nothing seemed to work, so I thought if I gave the ultimate sacrifice, my son, things would change, people would listen."

"Did it?"

"For a while, but then the same human flaws came to the surface: greed, pride, and envy. Let's change the subject to something a little less morbid, shall we?" he said.

"The fourth commandment says, Honor thy father and thy mother. Things have changed on Earth. Some families have two mothers or two fathers," she said and looked to him for his reaction, and he nodded.

"Some religious leaders on earth condemn the lifestyle and judge those people," Liz said.

"That's the problem with religions," he said and took a bite from the sandwich. She put her sandwich down and looked at God.

"Humans distort my words. Who appointed them judge? Certainly not me. Mathew had a great metaphor about it when he wrote, Why do you look at the splinter in your brother's eye and ignore the plank in your own eye? In other words, look at yourself first whenever you feel like judging others. The only judgment anyone has is the day you leave Earth; that job is mine. I almost wish there was another commandment, 'Don't judge others. It's not your job.' It really angers me sometimes. Sorry, I got carried away. You have a way of getting me to open up. You must have been a great attorney," he said.

Blushing, she said, "Thank you."

"What about the fourth commandment?" she asked.

"Liz, most young people ignore and disrespect their elders. There was a time when elders were held in a place of esteem for their knowledge. Sadly, that has changed. Elders, including your parents and grandparents, have a lifetime of experiences and wisdom learned from both their successes and failures. Many mistakes can be avoided by learning from the lessons of the older population. I don't want them to follow what the elders say blindly, but at least hear them out and thoughtfully consider what they say," he said.

"I have been guilty of not listening to my parents myself," Liz said.

"I think Mark Twain captured it perfectly when he said, When I was seventeen, I was convinced my father was a damn fool. When I was twenty-one, I was astounded at how much the old man learned in four years," God said.

Liz chuckled and asked, "How about Show respect for your elders? They know a lot more than you think?" Liz said.

"Perfect," God said.

God looked at Liz and asked, "No other questions today?"

"I do have one. Did you make the dinosaurs also?" she asked, and He nodded.

"They were the beta test while we figured out the logistics of populating the planet. Quite a bit goes into it. For example, did you know there are over 45,000 species of spiders alone? It took a long time to get the numbers right."

"You said we. Who else helped you?' she asked.

"The Holy Spirit. She is the details one. So organized," he said.

4th Commandment Ver 2.0 First draft

Show respect for your elders. They know a lot more than you think.

Thou shalt not kill

She played fetch in the yard with her dog Brady, a mixed breed her parents rescued when Liz was a child. Brady was the puppy she remembered; he even had the same white paws. He kissed her face until she giggled and slept beside her in bed, just like on Earth. She tossed the ball, and it bounced in front of God. He bent over to pick it up and petted Brady. He then softly tossed the ball, and Brady chased it down.

"How are you doing, Liz?" he asked.

"Great, thanks for asking. How are you?"

"Feeling a bit disjointed," he said, and they sat on the wooden steps to her cabin.

"Feel like talking?" she asked.

"The people on Earth are pulling further away. Evil is coursing through every part of society. I knew it would happen, of course, but I didn't realize how much it would hurt. I guess Lucifer's message resonates better than mine," he said.

Liz reached over and placed her hand on his, not saying anything, not knowing what to say.

"Why not just kill Lucifer?" she asked softly.

Taking a deep breath, he said, "I can't."

"You can't? You're God; pretty sure you can do anything,"

"The Fifth Commandment says Thou shalt not kill. I can't very well tell people not to kill, and then I kill Lucifer. It would make me a hypocrite. I would lose what trust I have left in the people. Secondly, humans have free will to choose good or evil. If I were to kill Lucifer, there would be no choice. Lucifer knows it and is ratcheting up the pressure, and they are listening to her message," he said.

"Wait, Lucifer is female?" she asked, and he nodded.

"It had to be that way; we are polar opposites, good and evil, male and female," he said.

"Never thought about it. Hopefully, things will change and return to normal," she said. He gave a half smile and nodded.

"Just curious why you chose me? So many others up here

are better qualified to do this, to edit the commandments," Liz asked.

"Why not you? Liz, you are an amazing soul. You are smart, funny, witty, and brave. When Jesus came to Earth, he didn't surround himself with the pillars of the communities, the respected scholars, and the teachers. He surrounded himself with ordinary people. Truth be told, I hate those pompous scholars who think they know everything. You understand the regular people," he said.

Blushing, she said, "Thank you."

"You're welcome," he said.

"So, the Fifth Commandment is simple: Thou shall not kill. I'm not sure it needs explaining or editing," she said.

"Yes, it is simple, and yet it isn't. Most people know they shouldn't murder someone, but they still do it at an alarming rate. Suicides are also spiking. Killing yourself is still killing," he said.

"What about capital punishment?" Liz asked.

"It's still murder, regardless of the pretense. The eye for an eye mentality is dangerous for society," he said.

"What about criminals?" she asked.

Shrugging, he said, "They should be jailed and will be judged when they leave Earth."

Liz asked, "How about every life is sacred, especially

yours?"

"I love it," he said.

"I do have another question. How come there are evil people in the world?" Liz asked.

"You asking about anyone in particular?" he asked.

"Miss Wilkerson, my eighth-grade teacher, was so mean all the time, and not just to me, she was mean to everyone," she said.

Sometimes, you must look at the back story to understand their actions. People become hardened by their circumstances. You remember Mr. Thompson?" God asked.

"My next-door neighbor?" she asked, and he nodded.

"He lost his brother and sister in a boating accident as a child. He was never the same, never opened his heart, never married, died an angry old man," God said, and she nodded.

"What about Miss Wilkerson? What's her back story?" Liz asked.

"Oh, there is no back story; she was evil and still is. Luckily, It's not our problem. Lucifer has to deal with her," he said.

5th Commandment Ver 2.0 First draft

Every life is sacred, especially yours.

Thou shalt not commit adultery.

Liz hiked through the woods and came to the clearing. She saw God seated on the creek's bank with his feet in the water. His eyes were closed, and he was facing the sun. As she stepped closer, God said, "Hello, Liz, thanks for coming here. This is one of my favorite places,"

"It is so serene," she said.

"Come sit," he said, patting the ground beside him. Liz kicked off her shoes and sat, slipping her feet into the cool water.

"I could get used to this," she said.

"Right," he said, smiling.

As she was about to say something, he raised his hand and said, "Just feel it."

Liz closed her eyes, the sun radiating onto her face and

skin, which felt amazing. A moment later, God said, "So which commandment are we on now?"

"Six," she replied.

"Thou shall not commit adultery," he said, and she nodded.

"What do you think about this one?" he asked and turned to face her. Her face reddened, and she softly said, "I cheated on my husband. I'm not proud of it. It was the final event that ended our marriage. I will never forget the hurt I saw in his face when I told him."

God reached over and took her hand, and she felt a warmness filling her body. Tears streamed from her eyes, and then happiness and joy filled her.

"Thank you," she said softly.

"Marriages used to be arranged, and it was more like a business agreement between families, but there was a sort of permanence. There was no love there, and the husband and wife were miserable. Society used to be quite harsh to adulterers. Couples were forced to stay together for fear of being ostracized in the community or worse," God said, and she nodded.

 "I never wanted marriages to be like a life sentence. I want humans to be happy and excited to be alive. So, I was pleased when it evolved from being a business arrangement to a marriage based on love. I then realized a marriage based on love is not happier than an arranged one," God said.

"Why is that?"

"I believe humans don't feel the joy inside themselves and look outside to find it, but that joy is fleeting and without a foundation," he said.

"What can they do?" she asked.

"Some of the finest minds in the world have debated this without resolve," he said, shaking his head.

"When couples are in the newlywed stage, they put each other as their top priority. Then life gets in the way," she said, trailing off.

"I think you have something there," God said.

Suddenly, Liz said, "How about this: Your spouse is your top priority, above career, family, hobbies, anything."

Smiling, God said, "I love it. If each spouse keeps the other as their top priority, then everything else falls into place."

"I just finished reading the bible, cover to cover. Most of it was understandable, but wow, the first and last books. Genesis started off OK, but then Moses went off the deep end, talking about people living for hundreds of years. He has an entire chapter on who was related to whom. And in Revelations, John talks about the end times and crazy stuff like seals opening and horses. It was bizarre," she said.

God chuckled and said, "Moses and John got hold of some "shrooms" while writing those chapters."

"Shrooms, as in magic mushrooms?" she asked, and God nodded.

"Which explains it. Sorry, one more question: why will you destroy the world? I can't wrap my head around it. You preach love," Liz asked, looking at God.

He stood and said, "I'm not going to do it, you are. Not you specifically, but humans will destroy the Earth with nuclear wars and bioweapons."

"When?" she asked, a tear in her eye and God shrugged his shoulders. "There is still a chance they will come to their senses," he said.

6th Commandment Ver 2.0 First draft

Your spouse is your top priority, above career, family, hobbies, anything.

Thou shall not steal

Liz was waiting outside her cabin when she saw the red convertible car pulling up the driveway. It was a 1960 Corvette Stingray with wide whitewall tires. The car had a vanity plate that read, Gods Vette.

When it stopped, she said, "This is really nice."

"It's my baby. Don't tell Jesus I called it that," he laughed.

"Your secret is safe with me," she said and sat inside and closed the door.

"Heard you went to the festival last night," he said. The festival was a celebration featuring crafts, rides, and games of skill.

"I did; it was fun. I even rode the Ferris Wheel," she said, proud of herself for overcoming her fear of heights.

"That's fun. George helped design it. Such a smart guy," he said.

"George, as in the George Ferris, the inventor of the Ferris Wheel?" she asked, and God nodded.

They stopped for an ice cream cone and God got a heavenly hash cone, and Liz got a soft serve of vanilla covered in chocolate.

 She followed God to a remote picnic table, and they sat atop it.

"So, Thou shall not steal," he said, and she nodded.

"It's short and to the point," she said.

"It is, and it isn't. I know I sound like a politician; allow me to explain. People start off small, stealing office supplies or fudging their timesheets, adding hours they didn't work. Conversely, employers steal from employees by not paying them their value. Now shoplifters and looters steal from stores, and the authorities look the other way, almost condoning it," he said.

"Some poor people steal food for their families."

"I get it, but when I see them walking out of stores with 85" TVs, expensive jewelry, or carjacking someone's car, I draw the line. It's like people have forgotten what is right and what is wrong," he said.

An idea popped into her head. "How about this? If you

didn't buy, rent, or inherit it, it's not yours. Don't take it. It doesn't belong to you."

"Sounds perfect," he said.

"I do have a question for you," he said, and she nodded and looked at God.

"In all seriousness, I would love if people thanked me for when things are going well in their life. Would it kill them to say Thanks God?"

"I agree 100%," she said.

Looking at God, she asked, "So looking back, what would you have changed when designing humans?"

Thinking for a moment, God said, "I would have offered extended warranties."

"Extended warranties?" she laughed.

"Yes I got the idea from James Wheeler and Richard Schulze, founders of Best Buy," God told her smiling broadly.

When they returned to his car, he sat in the passenger seat, and she looked at him. "Your turn. Don't wreck my baby," God said.

7th Commandment Ver 2.0 First draft

If you didn't buy, rent, or inherit it, it's not yours. Don't take it. It doesn't belong to you.

You shall not bear false witness against your neighbor.

Liz was excited about the concert. It was dubbed Heavens Legends Concert Series. It featured some of the most iconic musicians and singers ever. Today's concert featured three stars she never would have imagined on the same stage: Buddy Holly, Notorious BIG, and Wolfgang Amadeus Mozart. She danced in the grass the entire night to the eclectic music.

The next afternoon, she pedaled her bike to BC's Diner. Seated at an outdoor picnic table, the waitress placed a glass of sweet tea and a menu. As she was reading the menu, she smiled. The two chefs for the restaurant were Anthony Bourdain and Julia Child. As a girl, she remembered her mom watching Julia Child on TV.

A moment later, she heard the loud roar of a motorcycle. She looked up to see God arriving on a classic Harley

Davidson, the WLA. She remembered seeing a picture of one in her grandpa's garage.

"Beautiful day, isn't it?" he asked, and she nodded.

The waitress came to the table with an iced tea for God.

"How about that concert last night?"

"You were there?" Liz asked, and he nodded.

"It was awesome," she replied.

After placing their order, she said, "So, the 8th commandment."

"You shall not bear false witness against your neighbor," God said.

"I never really understood it," she admitted.

Shaking his head, God sipped his tea and said, "Not many do. They think it's about wrongfully accusing your neighbor of a crime. This entails much more. It includes gossiping about, slandering, or sowing doubt about another person. It is also meant for individuals who listen and judge fellow human beings by listening to the words of others. Once again, we must tell humans not to judge others. That gets under my craw."

The food arrived; God had a crab and seafood dish, and Liz chose the roasted chicken. It was amazing.

"Hello Dearie," they heard and saw Julia Child walking

briskly across the driveway with her blue apron. God stood and said, "Hello, Julia." They hugged, and he introduced Liz to Julia.

"How is everything?" Julia asked.

"Great as usual," God answered.

Liz said, "Amazing,"

"I need to get back inside. Robert is trying to add more wine. That boy is headstrong," she said and walked away.

As they sat, Liz said, "How about the minute you want to think or say something about another, remember your own shortcomings and work on those."

"Perfect, Liz," he said, and she smiled.

"Can I ask you a question?" Liz asked.

"Of course, anything?"

"You and Jesus are so different in your approach to humans. No offense, but you had some serious anger issues. Flooding the Earth, killing everyone but Noah and his family, plagues, locusts, droughts, and that whole thing of turning Lot's wife into salt. It seems like a bit of an overreaction. Meanwhile, Jesus is so different and not very flashy. He turned water into wine, and the only one who knew about the miracle was his mom, the fish and the loaves miracle, and paying the Roman taxes by finding a coin in the fish's mouth. Very low key."

God looked at Liz, rubbed his chin, and said, "I guess I was excessive. That whole tough love thing certainly backfired. I never thought of it that way. Thanks."

She smiled and said, "Welcome."

"Be careful on your bike on the way home," God said.

"Why is it going to rain?" she asked.

"Cloudy with a thirty percent chance of locusts," he said, driving away.

8th Commandment Ver 2.0 First draft

When you want to think or say something about another, remember your shortcomings and work on those.

Thou shall not covet thy neighbor's wife

Liz wore a sundress and straw hat to the afternoon Philosophy Round Table event. She and her grandmother Mary walked inside the amphitheater and found seats a few rows back. It was already crowded as many wanted to hear the speakers. It was a who's who of famous philosophers. Aristotle was the master of ceremonies and host. The others on the marquee were Plato, Socrates, and Confucius. The most amazing thing Liz found about Heaven was that she could understand everyone, their language and dialects, and they understood her when she spoke. After the event, Liz's grandmother asked if she wanted to get dinner. Liz politely declined and said she had a meeting.

She parked her 1969 Jeep Commando convertible in the restaurant's parking lot. It was the same model her grandfather had when she was a child. The sign on the restaurant was in Chinese, but she could read it. It read

Zuo and Peng, a restaurant for the people. Inside, she saw God at a booth, and he smiled. She noticed a short Asian man in the kitchen. Was he wearing a military outfit? she wondered.

"What's good here?" she asked.

"Pretty much everything. I usually get the General Tso's chicken, named after the owner."

"OK, I'll get it too. Did I see a man wearing a military uniform?" she asked.

"That's Zuo, or you would know him as General Tso. He is having a reunion with his friends."

"Really," she said excitedly.

"Yes, his real name is Zuo Zongtang, and he goes by General Tso."

"Hmm, I never knew. Did he invent the chicken dish named after him?" she asked.

"No, a chef named Peng Chang-kuei invented it. He's back there too. They get along now but when they first got here, there were some heated words. Zuo wanted to be known for his works and accomplishments and not for a chicken dish."

After eating, Liz said, "So, the 8th commandment."

"Thou shall not covet thy neighbor's wife," God said.

"This one is confusing as well. It doesn't mention husband and seems a bit one-sided," Liz said.

"Yeah, they missed the point altogether. I had them written on a tablet, and they still messed it up. If you look up the word Covet in the dictionary, it means to desire wrongly or without due regard for the rights of others. The commandment actually says you shall not covet your neighbor's house, wife, servant, ox, donkey, or anything that belongs to your neighbor. The whole point of this commandment is to be happy with what you have and not compare yourself to others. Sometimes, I hear the thoughts of people attending mass, envious of what the others in the church have, whether it's a good job, nice house, new car, or attractive spouse. They think these thoughts instead of listening to the sermon or gospel. It kinda frustrates me."

Liz nodded and said, "I could see that."

Thinking for a moment, she asked, "How about this? Be happy with your gifts and quit comparing your life to others. You never know what is going on behind their doors."

"I like it," he said.

"Can I ask a question?" Liz asked

"Of course."

"Women and men are so different. You put two incompatible species together and said, "There you go. Work it out," Liz said.

He laughed out loud, "It does appear like that."

"Did you do that on purpose?" she asked.

"The best-laid plans of Mice and Men"

"Robert Burns," she said, smiling.

Nodding, God said, "I deliberately made man and woman different, hoping it would produce a sort of synergism where the two together would be better than two apart. Wow, was I wrong?"

9th Commandment Ver 2.0 First draft

Be happy with your gifts and quit comparing your life to others.

Thou shall not covet thy neighbor's goods

Liz was seated at a table overlooking the lake. The water was so calm it almost looked like a mirror. She sipped her coffee and thought, Thank you God.

"You're welcome," she heard and turned to see God pull the chair across from her out and sit.

"Good morning," she said.

"Stunning morning, is it not?"

"Yes, it is," she answered.

God sipped his hot Earl Grey tea and said, "Doesn't it amaze you how people can look at scenes like this and never give it a second thought. You never did. I appreciate it."

"My mom taught me to try finding five things a day to be thankful for. I love days like today and am thankful to experience them," Liz said, and God smiled.

After a breakfast of French Toast for Liz and an omelet for God, she said, "Well, we are on the last commandment: Thou shall not covet the neighbors' goods. It seems a bit redundant of the seventh and ninth commandments."

Nodding, God said, "It is, and yet it needs to be repeated because no one seems to get it. Stealing is widespread in humans, and it pains me. Countries take from other countries. Corporations take from those without the means to fight back. Humans loot and steal, feeling entitled to whatever they take. This has happened since the beginning of time but now it's pervasive."

Liz smiled and asked, "How about something simple like an asterisk and say, "See Commandments 7 and 9."

"Very funny," he said, smiling.

"It's like learning the difference between envy and jealousy. Envy is wanting to be like your neighbor or relative and working to achieve it while jealousy is wishing you could take what they have for yourself," Liz said.

"That's a great way of putting it. Jealousy is the worst trait."

Liz looked out onto the lake and asked, "How about, It's OK to envy others, but don't be jealous of them."

"I like it," God said nodding.

"I have another question. You know me. Mathew 10:30

says even the very hairs of your head are numbered. Luke 21:18 says not a hair of your head will perish. If those are true, why are some men bald?" she asked, tongue in cheek.

Without missing a beat, God said, "There are only a few perfect male heads. The others I cover with hair."

She giggled, and they embraced.

Liz had a tear in her eye and said, "I guess this is it. We did all Ten Commandments. I'm going to miss our get-togethers."

God looked at Liz and asked, "What are you talking about? We just got started. I want to redo the Jewish commandments. They have 613 of them. Are you up for the challenge?"

"You bet," she said, beaming.

"Seeya next week, Counselor," he said and disappeared.

10th Commandment Ver 2.0 First draft

It's OK to envy others, but don't be jealous of them.

ABOUT THE AUTHOR

I grew up in the Catholic faith and my family only attended mass on Christmas and Easter. My parents sent me to a Catholic grade school. The nuns that taught there were like the fire and brimstone of the Old Testament. They would tell scary stories about God and his vengeance. As a child I was terrified of God and wondered why he was so mean if he loved us.

Later in life, my fiancé and then wife asked me to attend Sunday mass with her and her family. It was then when my faith started to grow. I became more involved with the church and started reading the bible. It helped me put into perspective the Sunday readings in church which only featured snippets of the chapters. I became a Eucharistic Minister at my church.

Hearing a sermon one day changed the way I prayed. The priest told the audience to start being thankful for the daily blessings and not just call on God when things were difficult. He suggested finding five things a day to be thankful of. Some days were easier than others, but I kept doing it. Then my life fell apart. My business and health were failing, and I was angry with God for allowing it to happen. Then a voice told me to attend church that evening. I argued with the voice and finally relented. Inside the church before the mass, I prayed to God and asked for help and guidance. A feeling enveloped me, and it was the most amazing feeling ever, like a giant hug. Then the voice said, "Everything will be ok. I love you." Tears streamed down my cheeks, and I knew everything was going to be ok. That was the one and only time I felt God reach out to me directly. I guess I needed that. Ever since then, I know God is there working in the background through others. Thank you, God.